Black Hole Paradox

Angela Strumpfer

Presentation by *BookLeaf Publishing*

Web: www.bookleafpub.com

E-mail: info@bookleafpub.com

ISBN: 9789357610490

First edition 2022

DEDICATION

For those looking for light to feel understood,

And to my light,

My Jeremy

ACKNOWLEDGEMENT

Foremost, my infamous debate coach who dry cleaned his jeans and had "shut up and color day" when we were all too much. Through his simple observations and encouragement, he provided a safe place for me to explore myself.

My personal therapist, my friend Laura who never stops asking me how things make me feel. Due to her constant inquisition, I have learned to continue exploring even in the face of pain.

My partner in crime, my friend Jordan who showed me his world and accepted me with open arms when I discovered the missing pieces in mine. You helped me find myself again.

My person, Jeremy. Your presence in my life has moved mountains. Knowing you exist helped me to swim the widest seas. Your soul speaks to mine. I am forever grateful for the conversation.

Lastly, my parents and siblings for making sure I made it to adulthood in one piece. Through your love, laughter and encouragement I have blossomed. Who would have ever thought?

PREFACE

Unlike EE Cummings, I insist these poems are meant for everyone. Their very intent is connection. I wrote them with this weighing heavy on my shoulder like a mountain. If one person finds the words for their state of being, they will have served their intent. The mountain will settle into boulders and roll off my back.

To me, life is connection. Sweet goes with salty (don't even try to change my mind), the sea marries land at the horizon, rain rhythmically combines with pine, your experience connects with mine. This happens in minuscule and magnanimous ways. This connection brought me home. This connection kept me alive. Through my darkest times it has always provided a light.

In short quips, this anthology delves into my inner world. I hold up a light, so that we may create even in darkness, the inescapable beauty of our connection. I will burn in hopes of bringing others home. In dream of keeping another alive.

Let us all burn in the light of reciprocity.

Before It Breaks

Say something,

Anything,

Take a breath and form the words.

Don't worry about placing your shaky hands in
your pockets,

As you don't want to break all the delicates.

Your voice will shatter them all.

So say something,

Anything,

Be free to let your inner world out.

Don't worry about the aftermath,

It is a safe harbor here.

Whatever delicates break in the expression,

Were not yours to care for.

Affliction

Solitary.

Withstanding all silence,

I wearily stand to face the darkness.

Innately I know all facets evolve,

Anticipation for the light,

Delivering me,

From affliction.

Silent Articulation

Do not attach yourself.

My body is composed of wishbones,

My heart is a glass mosaic,

In physical form I am weak,

Delicate,

Fragile.

Rather come to me in silent articulation.

For my spirit is robust.

My soul,

Worthy of your tending.

Luminary Guide

Been fading for so long,

I'm lost completely.

What will switch me on again?

So inner illumine can form an outline,

Transforming darkness into light.

My luminary guide,

Leading me back,

Towards myself.

Personal Arsenic

The past which comes along with me is not an easy pill to swallow.

It chokes all who attempt it.

My personal arsenic.

No one is immune.

Fireproof Box

Ablaze with passion,

Contained.

Does anyone see within?

My presence speaks of normality,

Yet my glassy eyes,

Wavering voice,

And clenched hands tell of the depths.

An unseen soul,

Locked within perceptions,

Alternate versions of a singular being.

None,

Accurate.

City Skyline

I have so much to say to you,

Sharp,

Momentous,

Threatening to burst forth from expansion,

It remains lodged in my chest like a skyscraper,

Turning my chest into a city skyline,

Ablaze with the light of you.

Talking To Walls

Spent some time talking to walls.

Concrete,

Brick,

Human are all the same.

Absorbing all meaning.

Never reciprocating emotion.

Leaving me wanting,

Haunted,

And forlorn.

The Power Of Choice

Choices,

Your existence my saving grace.

Suffering eases.

Opportunity knocks.

Change ushers in as a new dawn breaks.

You have rescued me from myself,

Instigating rebirth within a barren soulscape.

Weights And Wings

There is a weight I carry,

Vast and relentless,

It's restraint unyielding.

My soul has yet to buckle under pressure,

But it comes close,

The debauchery of the present excessive,

Mankind discounting it's true nature.

At these times,

I look toward nature.

Wildflowers breaking through cement.

A bird's nest wrapped around a telephone pole.

I take witness to nature's finesse,

An ability to grow despite environment.

I draw this knowledge in,

Spread my soul's wings,

And attempt to fly.

Purgatory

I am a restless spirit,

Knowing exactly where I belong,

Not yet allowed to reside there.

I am contained in a state of limbo...

My previous lifestyle no longer an option,

My future not presently obtainable.

Glassblower

I don't want what's not mine,

Yet I yearn.

An ember burns,

Glowing through the darkness,

Reminding me of the light.

You have taken up residence like a glassblower
employing fire to your will.

Alternate Me

I long to be the color of pleasure,

To radiate an aura of self contentment.

I long to possess a boisterous spirit,

To empower the curiosity found in outsiders.

I long...

Long to create...

An alternate me.

Within

15

I am an ever changing current.

A river that floods the washes in the spring.

I change the landscape around me unknowingly.

I have evolved from my trickle,

Filled with winter's run off,

Overflowing with the new abundance of the universe.

My soul has patiently awaited precipitation to wash away old foundations,

Knowing one must begin at the core,

The true nature found within.

Wearing My Past

I wrote a letter to the rain,

Asking to cleanse my muddled past…

I received no reply.

So it clings,

like a threadbare coat,

cloaking my every intention.

Bellows

Inside,

I stir.

Awakened by the fire in your words.

I search.

Not for water,

Not for escape,

Yet rather a bellows,

To burst ember into flame.

Use me as kindling.

 I wish to be ablaze.

Incandescent.

Sweltering in the light of your presence.

Asking The Serious Questions

I reach out in uncertainty,

Vast emptiness reaches back,

I have become skilled in the lack of reciprocity,

A solitary front withstanding all silence.

Weaver Wanted

Weaver wanted.

Thread the light into my dark tapestry of soul.

Set me afire.

Ablaze in beauty.

Aglow through the light of your love.

Letting Go

Grasping on to glimpses of my unruly youth,

Not yet secure enough to set them free.

Glancing back at the whispers of whom I used to be,

Frightened of the reflection I now perceive.

Musings Of Cloudwalking

Sweet melody on tip of tongue,

Bursting forth.

Harmonizing.

If only in the mind.

I dance here amongst the notes,

Soul stirring.

Relentless.

Moved beyond boundaries.

It is here I thrive,

Amplified,

Like my wildly vivid dreams.

Intimate Correspondence In
The Height Of Summer

I am exposed.

My inner world draped across my flesh like a
massive cloak.

Covering all normalcy.